My
Travel Journal

_____

DATE: _____ PLACE: _____

HOW I FELT TODAY:

WHAT I'VE SEEN TODAY:

_____
_____
_____
_____
_____
_____
_____
_____
_____
_____
_____
_____

WHAT I ATE TODAY:

_____
_____
_____
_____
_____

HOW DID WE TRAVEL:

THE BEST THING THAT HAPPENED TOODAY:

_____
_____

THE WEATHER TODAY WAS:

PLACE FOR DRAWINGS, PAINTINGS, WRITING, ENTRY TICKETS, PICTURES OR ALL THE OTHER STUFF YOU WANT TO CAPTURE

Date: Place:

How I felt Today:

What I've Seen today:

_____
_____
_____
_____
_____
_____
_____
_____
_____
_____

What I Ate Today:

_____
_____
_____
_____
_____

How did we Travel:

The Best Thing that happened tooday:
_____
_____

THe Weather today was:

PLACE FOR DRAWINGS, PAINTINGS, WRITING, ENTRY TICKETS, PICTURES OR ALL THE OTHER STUFF YOU WANT TO CAPTURE

Date: | Place:

How I felt Today:

What I've Seen today:	What I Ate Today:
_____	_____
_____	_____
_____	_____
_____	_____
_____	_____
_____	**How did we Travel:**
_____	
_____	
_____	
_____	

The Best Thing that happened tooday:
_____
_____

The Weather today was:

PLACE FOR DRAWINGS, PAINTINGS, WRITING, ENTRY TICKETS, PICTURES OR ALL THE OTHER STUFF YOU WANT TO CAPTURE

DATE: _____   PLACE: _____

HOW I FELT TODAY:

WHAT I'VE SEEN TODAY:

_____
_____
_____
_____
_____
_____
_____
_____
_____
_____
_____

WHAT I ATE TODAY:

_____
_____
_____
_____
_____

HOW DID WE TRAVEL:

THE BEST THING THAT HAPPENED TOODAY:

_____
_____

THE WEATHER TODAY WAS:

PLACE FOR DRAWINGS, PAINTINGS, WRITING, ENTRY TICKETS, PICTURES OR ALL THE OTHER STUFF YOU WANT TO CAPTURE

Date: | Place:

How I felt Today:

What I've Seen today:

_____
_____
_____
_____
_____
_____
_____
_____
_____
_____
_____

What I Ate Today:

_____
_____
_____
_____
_____

How did we Travel:

The Best Thing that happened tooday:

_____
_____

The Weather today was:

PLACE FOR DRAWINGS, PAINTINGS, WRITING, ENTRY TICKETS, PICTURES OR ALL THE OTHER STUFF YOU WANT TO CAPTURE

DATE: _____ PLACE: _____

HOW I FELT TODAY:

WHAT I'VE SEEN TODAY:

_____
_____
_____
_____
_____
_____
_____
_____
_____
_____
_____

WHAT I ATE TODAY:

_____
_____
_____
_____
_____

HOW DID WE TRAVEL:

THE BEST THING THAT HAPPENED TOODAY:

_____
_____

THE WEATHER TODAY WAS:

PLACE FOR DRAWINGS, PAINTINGS, WRITING, ENTRY TICKETS, PICTURES OR ALL THE OTHER STUFF YOU WANT TO CAPTURE

Date:

Place:

How I felt Today:

What I've Seen today:	What I Ate Today:
_____	_____
_____	_____
_____	_____
_____	_____
_____	_____
_____	_____
_____	**How did we Travel:**
_____	
_____	
_____	
_____	
_____	

The Best Thing that happened tooday:
_____
_____

The Weather today was:

PLACE FOR DRAWINGS, PAINTINGS, WRITING, ENTRY TICKETS, PICTURES OR ALL THE OTHER STUFF YOU WANT TO CAPTURE

DATE: : PLACE:

HOW I FELT TODAY:

WHAT I'VE SEEN TODAY:

_____
_____
_____
_____
_____
_____
_____
_____
_____
_____
_____
_____

WHAT I ATE TODAY:

_____
_____
_____
_____
_____

HOW DID WE TRAVEL:

THE BEST THING THAT HAPPENED TOODAY:
_____
_____

THE WEATHER TODAY WAS:

PLACE FOR DRAWINGS, PAINTINGS, WRITING, ENTRY TICKETS, PICTURES OR ALL THE OTHER STUFF YOU WANT TO CAPTURE

DATE: _____ | PLACE: _____

HOW I FELT TODAY:

WHAT I'VE SEEN TODAY:

_____
_____
_____
_____
_____
_____
_____
_____
_____
_____
_____
_____

WHAT I ATE TODAY:

_____
_____
_____
_____

HOW DID WE TRAVEL:

THE BEST THING THAT HAPPENED TOODAY:

_____
_____

THE WEATHER TODAY WAS:

PLACE FOR DRAWINGS, PAINTINGS, WRITING, ENTRY TICKETS, PICTURES OR ALL THE OTHER STUFF YOU WANT TO CAPTURE

DATE: _____ PLACE: _____

HOW I FELT TODAY:

😀 🙂 😐 😎 😎 😫

WHAT I'VE SEEN TODAY:

_____
_____
_____
_____
_____
_____
_____
_____
_____
_____
_____
_____

WHAT I ATE TODAY:

_____
_____
_____
_____
_____

HOW DID WE TRAVEL:

THE BEST THING THAT HAPPENED TOODAY:

_____
_____

THE WEATHER TODAY WAS:

PLACE FOR DRAWINGS, PAINTINGS, WRITING, ENTRY TICKETS, PICTURES OR ALL THE OTHER STUFF YOU WANT TO CAPTURE

DATE: PLACE:

HOW I FELT TODAY:

WHAT I'VE SEEN TODAY:

_____
_____
_____
_____
_____
_____
_____
_____
_____
_____
_____
_____

WHAT I ATE TODAY:

_____
_____
_____
_____
_____

HOW DID WE TRAVEL:

THE BEST THING THAT HAPPENED TOODAY:
_____
_____

THE WEATHER TODAY WAS:

PLACE FOR DRAWINGS, PAINTINGS, WRITING, ENTRY TICKETS, PICTURES OR ALL THE OTHER STUFF YOU WANT TO CAPTURE

DATE: PLACE:

HOW I FELT TODAY:

WHAT I'VE SEEN TODAY:

_____
_____
_____
_____
_____
_____
_____
_____
_____
_____
_____

WHAT I ATE TODAY:

_____
_____
_____
_____
_____

HOW DID WE TRAVEL:

THE BEST THING THAT HAPPENED TOODAY:
_____
_____

THE WEATHER TODAY WAS:

PLACE FOR DRAWINGS, PAINTINGS, WRITING, ENTRY TICKETS, PICTURES OR ALL THE OTHER STUFF YOU WANT TO CAPTURE

DATE: _____   PLACE: _____

HOW I FELT TODAY:

WHAT I'VE SEEN TODAY:
_____
_____
_____
_____
_____
_____
_____
_____
_____
_____
_____
_____

WHAT I ATE TODAY:
_____
_____
_____
_____
_____

HOW DID WE TRAVEL:

THE BEST THING THAT HAPPENED TOODAY:
_____
_____

THE WEATHER TODAY WAS:

PLACE FOR DRAWINGS, PAINTINGS, WRITING, ENTRY TICKETS, PICTURES OR ALL THE OTHER STUFF YOU WANT TO CAPTURE

DATE: _____   PLACE: _____

HOW I FELT TODAY:

WHAT I'VE SEEN TODAY:	WHAT I ATE TODAY:
_____	_____
_____	_____
_____	_____
_____	_____
_____	
_____	HOW DID WE TRAVEL:
_____	
_____	
_____	
_____	

THE BEST THING THAT HAPPENED TOODAY:
_____
_____

THE WEATHER TODAY WAS:

PLACE FOR DRAWINGS, PAINTINGS, WRITING, ENTRY TICKETS, PICTURES OR ALL THE OTHER STUFF YOU WANT TO CAPTURE

Date: _____ Place: _____

How I felt Today:

What I've Seen today:
_____
_____
_____
_____
_____
_____
_____
_____
_____
_____
_____

What I Ate Today:
_____
_____
_____
_____
_____

How did we Travel:

The Best Thing that happened tooday:
_____
_____

The Weather today was:

PlacE foR DRAWINGS, PAINTINGS, WRITING, ENTRY TICKETS, PICTURES OR ALL THE OTHER STUFF YOU WANT TO CAPTURE

DATE: PLACE:

HOW I FELT TODAY:

WHAT I'VE SEEN TODAY:

_____
_____
_____
_____
_____
_____
_____
_____
_____
_____
_____

WHAT I ATE TODAY:

_____
_____
_____
_____

HOW DID WE TRAVEL:

THE BEST THING THAT HAPPENED TOODAY:
_____
_____

THE WEATHER TODAY WAS:

PLACE FOR DRAWINGS, PAINTINGS, WRITING, ENTRY TICKETS, PICTURES OR ALL THE OTHER STUFF YOU WANT TO CAPTURE

DATE: .... | PLACE: ....

HOW I FELT TODAY:

WHAT I'VE SEEN TODAY:

_____
_____
_____
_____
_____
_____
_____
_____
_____
_____
_____
_____

WHAT I ATE TODAY:

_____
_____
_____
_____
_____

HOW DID WE TRAVEL:

THE BEST THING THAT HAPPENED TOODAY:

_____
_____

THE WEATHER TODAY WAS:

PLACE FOR DRAWINGS, PAINTINGS, WRITING, ENTRY TICKETS, PICTURES OR ALL THE OTHER STUFF YOU WANT TO CAPTURE

DATE: .... PLACE: ....

HOW I FELT TODAY:

WHAT I'VE SEEN TODAY:

_____
_____
_____
_____
_____
_____
_____
_____
_____
_____
_____

WHAT I ATE TODAY:

_____
_____
_____
_____
_____

HOW DID WE TRAVEL:

THE BEST THING THAT HAPPENED TOODAY:

_____
_____

THE WEATHER TODAY WAS:

PLACE FOR DRAWINGS, PAINTINGS, WRITING, ENTRY TICKETS, PICTURES OR ALL THE OTHER STUFF YOU WANT TO CAPTURE

DATE: _____   PLACE: _____

HOW I FELT TODAY:

WHAT I'VE SEEN TODAY:

_____
_____
_____
_____
_____
_____
_____
_____
_____
_____
_____
_____

WHAT I ATE TODAY:

_____
_____
_____
_____
_____

HOW DID WE TRAVEL:

THE BEST THING THAT HAPPENED TOODAY:

_____
_____

THE WEATHER TODAY WAS:

PLACE FOR DRAWINGS, PAINTINGS, WRITING, ENTRY TICKETS, PICTURES OR ALL THE OTHER STUFF YOU WANT TO CAPTURE

DATE: _____ PLACE: _____

HOW I FELT TODAY:

WHAT I'VE SEEN TODAY:

_____
_____
_____
_____
_____
_____
_____
_____
_____
_____
_____

WHAT I ATE TODAY:

_____
_____
_____
_____
_____

HOW DID WE TRAVEL:

THE BEST THING THAT HAPPENED TOODAY:
_____
_____

THE WEATHER TODAY WAS:

PLACE FOR DRAWINGS, PAINTINGS, WRITING, ENTRY TICKETS, PICTURES OR ALL THE OTHER STUFF YOU WANT TO CAPTURE

DATE: PLACE:

HOW I FELT TODAY:

WHAT I'VE SEEN TODAY:

_____
_____
_____
_____
_____
_____
_____
_____
_____
_____
_____
_____

WHAT I ATE TODAY:

_____
_____
_____
_____

HOW DID WE TRAVEL:

THE BEST THING THAT HAPPENED TOODAY:
_____
_____

THE WEATHER TODAY WAS:

PLACE FOR DRAWINGS, PAINTINGS, WRITING, ENTRY TICKETS, PICTURES OR ALL THE OTHER STUFF YOU WANT TO CAPTURE

DATE: _____ PLACE: _____

HOW I FELT TODAY:

WHAT I'VE SEEN TODAY:

_____
_____
_____
_____
_____
_____
_____
_____
_____
_____
_____

WHAT I ATE TODAY:

_____
_____
_____
_____
_____

HOW DID WE TRAVEL:

THE BEST THING THAT HAPPENED TOODAY:

_____
_____

THE WEATHER TODAY WAS:

PLACE FOR DRAWINGS, PAINTINGS, WRITING, ENTRY TICKETS, PICTURES OR ALL THE OTHER STUFF YOU WANT TO CAPTURE

Date: Place:

How I felt Today:

What I've Seen today:

_____
_____
_____
_____
_____
_____
_____
_____
_____
_____
_____
_____

What I Ate Today:

_____
_____
_____
_____
_____

How did we Travel:

The Best Thing that happened tooday:

_____
_____

The Weather today was:

PlACf fOR DRAWINGS, PAINTINGS, WRITING, ENTRY TICKETS, PICTURES OR ALL THE OTHER STUFF YOU WANT TO CAPTURE

DATE: PLACE:

HOW I FELT TODAY:

WHAT I'VE SEEN TODAY:

_____
_____
_____
_____
_____
_____
_____
_____
_____
_____
_____
_____

WHAT I ATE TODAY:

_____
_____
_____
_____

HOW DID WE TRAVEL:

THE BEST THING THAT HAPPENED TOODAY:

_____
_____

THE WEATHER TODAY WAS:

PLACE FOR DRAWINGS, PAINTINGS, WRITING, ENTRY TICKETS, PICTURES OR ALL THE OTHER STUFF YOU WANT TO CAPTURE

DATE: PLACE:

HOW I FELT TODAY:

WHAT I'VE SEEN TODAY:

_____
_____
_____
_____
_____
_____
_____
_____
_____
_____
_____

WHAT I ATE TODAY:

_____
_____
_____
_____

HOW DID WE TRAVEL:

THE BEST THING THAT HAPPENED TOODAY:

_____
_____

THE WEATHER TODAY WAS:

PLACE FOR DRAWINGS, PAINTINGS, WRITING, ENTRY TICKETS, PICTURES OR ALL THE OTHER STUFF YOU WANT TO CAPTURE

DATE: .... PLACE: ....

HOW I FELT TODAY:

WHAT I'VE SEEN TODAY:

_____
_____
_____
_____
_____
_____
_____
_____
_____
_____
_____
_____

WHAT I ATE TODAY:

_____
_____
_____
_____
_____

HOW DID WE TRAVEL:

THE BEST THING THAT HAPPENED TOODAY:

_____
_____

THE WEATHER TODAY WAS:

PLACE FOR DRAWINGS, PAINTINGS, WRITING, ENTRY TICKETS, PICTURES OR ALL THE OTHER STUFF YOU WANT TO CAPTURE

DATE: _____ | PLACE: _____

HOW I FELT TODAY:

WHAT I'VE SEEN TODAY:
_____
_____
_____
_____
_____
_____
_____
_____
_____
_____
_____
_____

WHAT I ATE TODAY:
_____
_____
_____
_____
_____

HOW DID WE TRAVEL:

THE BEST THING THAT HAPPENED TOODAY:
_____
_____

THE WEATHER TODAY WAS:

PlACE FOR DRAWINGS, PAINTINGS, WRITING, ENTRY TICKETS, PICTURES OR ALL THE OTHER STUFF YOU WANT TO CAPTURE

DATE: PLACE:

HOW I FELT TODAY:

WHAT I'VE SEEN TODAY:

_____
_____
_____
_____
_____
_____
_____
_____
_____
_____
_____
_____

WHAT I ATE TODAY:

_____
_____
_____
_____
_____

HOW DID WE TRAVEL:

THE BEST THING THAT HAPPENED TOODAY:

_____
_____

THE WEATHER TODAY WAS:

PLACE FOR DRAWINGS, PAINTINGS, WRITING, ENTRY TICKETS, PICTURES OR ALL THE OTHER STUFF YOU WANT TO CAPTURE

DATE: PLACE:

HOW I FELT TODAY:

WHAT I'VE SEEN TODAY:

_____
_____
_____
_____
_____
_____
_____
_____
_____
_____
_____
_____

WHAT I ATE TODAY:

_____
_____
_____
_____

HOW DID WE TRAVEL:

THE BEST THING THAT HAPPENED TOODAY:

_____
_____

THE WEATHER TODAY WAS:

PLACE FOR DRAWINGS, PAINTINGS, WRITING, ENTRY TICKETS, PICTURES OR ALL THE OTHER STUFF YOU WANT TO CAPTURE

DATE: **PLACE:**

HOW I FELT TODAY:

WHAT I'VE SEEN TODAY:

_____
_____
_____
_____
_____
_____
_____
_____
_____
_____
_____
_____

WHAT I ATE TODAY:

_____
_____
_____
_____

HOW DID WE TRAVEL:

THE BEST THING THAT HAPPENED TOODAY:
_____
_____

THE WEATHER TODAY WAS:

PLACE FOR DRAWINGS, PAINTINGS, WRITING, ENTRY TICKETS, PICTURES OR ALL THE OTHER STUFF YOU WANT TO CAPTURE

DATE: _____ PLACE: _____

HOW I FELT TODAY:

WHAT I'VE SEEN TODAY:	WHAT I ATE TODAY:
_____	_____
_____	_____
_____	_____
_____	_____
_____	HOW DID WE TRAVEL:
_____	
_____	
_____	
_____	
_____	
_____	

THE BEST THING THAT HAPPENED TOODAY:
_____
_____

THE WEATHER TODAY WAS:

PLACE FOR DRAWINGS, PAINTINGS, WRITING, ENTRY TICKETS, PICTURES OR ALL THE OTHER STUFF YOU WANT TO CAPTURE

Date: _____ | Place: _____

How I felt Today:

What I've Seen today:

_____
_____
_____
_____
_____
_____
_____
_____
_____
_____
_____
_____
_____

What I Ate Today:

_____
_____
_____
_____
_____

How did we Travel:

The Best Thing that happened tooday:

_____
_____

The Weather today was:

PLACE FOR DRAWINGS, PAINTINGS, WRITING, ENTRY TICKETS, PICTURES OR ALL THE OTHER STUFF YOU WANT TO CAPTURE

Date: _____ | Place: _____

How I felt Today:

What I've Seen today:
_____
_____
_____
_____
_____
_____
_____
_____
_____
_____
_____
_____

What I Ate Today:
_____
_____
_____
_____

How did we Travel:

The Best Thing that happened tooday:
_____
_____

THe Weather today was:

PLACE FOR DRAWINGS, PAINTINGS, WRITING, ENTRY TICKETS, PICTURES OR ALL THE OTHER STUFF YOU WANT TO CAPTURE

DATE: _____ PLACE: _____

HOW I FELT TODAY:

WHAT I'VE SEEN TODAY:

_____
_____
_____
_____
_____
_____
_____
_____
_____
_____
_____
_____

WHAT I ATE TODAY:

_____
_____
_____
_____
_____

HOW DID WE TRAVEL:

THE BEST THING THAT HAPPENED TOODAY:

_____
_____

THE WEATHER TODAY WAS:

PLACE FOR DRAWINGS, PAINTINGS, WRITING, ENTRY TICKETS, PICTURES OR ALL THE OTHER STUFF YOU WANT TO CAPTURE

DATE: | PLACE:

HOW I FELT TODAY:

WHAT I'VE SEEN TODAY:

_____
_____
_____
_____
_____
_____
_____
_____
_____
_____
_____

WHAT I ATE TODAY:

_____
_____
_____
_____

HOW DID WE TRAVEL:

THE BEST THING THAT HAPPENED TOODAY:

_____
_____

THE WEATHER TODAY WAS:

PLACE FOR DRAWINGS, PAINTINGS, WRITING, ENTRY TICKETS, PICTURES OR ALL THE OTHER STUFF YOU WANT TO CAPTURE

Date: Place:

How I felt Today:

What I've Seen today:
_____
_____
_____
_____
_____
_____
_____
_____
_____
_____
_____
_____

What I Ate Today:
_____
_____
_____
_____

How did we Travel:

The Best Thing that happened tooday:
_____
_____

The Weather today was:

PLACE FOR DRAWINGS, PAINTINGS, WRITING, ENTRY TICKETS, PICTURES OR ALL THE OTHER STUFF YOU WANT TO CAPTURE

Date: _____   Place: _____

How I felt Today:

What I've Seen today:

_____
_____
_____
_____
_____
_____
_____
_____
_____
_____
_____

What I Ate Today:

_____
_____
_____
_____

How did we Travel:

The Best Thing that happened tooday:

_____
_____

The Weather today was:

PLACE FOR DRAWINGS, PAINTINGS, WRITING, ENTRY TICKETS, PICTURES OR ALL THE OTHER STUFF YOU WANT TO CAPTURE

Date: | Place:

How I felt Today:

What I've Seen today:

_____
_____
_____
_____
_____
_____
_____
_____
_____
_____
_____

What I Ate Today:

_____
_____
_____
_____
_____

How did we Travel:

The Best Thing that happened tooday:

_____
_____

The Weather today was:

PLACE FOR DRAWINGS, PAINTINGS, WRITING, ENTRY TICKETS, PICTURES OR ALL THE OTHER STUFF YOU WANT TO CAPTURE

DATE: PLACE:

HOW I FELT TODAY:

WHAT I'VE SEEN TODAY:

_____
_____
_____
_____
_____
_____
_____
_____
_____
_____
_____

WHAT I ATE TODAY:

_____
_____
_____
_____

HOW DID WE TRAVEL:

THE BEST THING THAT HAPPENED TOODAY:
_____
_____

THE WEATHER TODAY WAS:

PLACE FOR DRAWINGS, PAINTINGS, WRITING, ENTRY TICKETS, PICTURES OR ALL THE OTHER STUFF YOU WANT TO CAPTURE

DATE: _____   PLACE: _____

HOW I FELT TODAY:

WHAT I'VE SEEN TODAY:
_____
_____
_____
_____
_____
_____
_____
_____
_____
_____
_____
_____

WHAT I ATE TODAY:
_____
_____
_____
_____
_____

HOW DID WE TRAVEL:

THE BEST THING THAT HAPPENED TOODAY:
_____
_____

THE WEATHER TODAY WAS:

PLACE FOR DRAWINGS, PAINTINGS, WRITING, ENTRY TICKETS, PICTURES OR ALL THE OTHER STUFF YOU WANT TO CAPTURE

DATE: _____   PLACE: _____

HOW I FELT TODAY:

WHAT I'VE SEEN TODAY:

_____
_____
_____
_____
_____
_____
_____
_____
_____
_____
_____
_____

WHAT I ATE TODAY:

_____
_____
_____
_____

HOW DID WE TRAVEL:

THE BEST THING THAT HAPPENED TOODAY:

_____
_____

THE WEATHER TODAY WAS:

PLACE FOR DRAWINGS, PAINTINGS, WRITING, ENTRY TICKETS, PICTURES OR ALL THE OTHER STUFF YOU WANT TO CAPTURE

Date: _____ Place: _____

How I felt Today:

What I've Seen today:

_____
_____
_____
_____
_____
_____
_____
_____
_____
_____
_____
_____

What I Ate Today:

_____
_____
_____
_____

How did we Travel:

The Best Thing that happened tooday:

_____
_____

The Weather today was:

PLACE FOR DRAWINGS, PAINTINGS, WRITING, ENTRY TICKETS, PICTURES OR ALL THE OTHER STUFF YOU WANT TO CAPTURE

DATE: PLACE:

HOW I FELT TODAY:

WHAT I'VE SEEN TODAY:

_____
_____
_____
_____
_____
_____
_____
_____
_____
_____

WHAT I ATE TODAY:

_____
_____
_____
_____

HOW DID WE TRAVEL:

THE BEST THING THAT HAPPENED TOODAY:

_____
_____

THE WEATHER TODAY WAS:

PLACE FOR DRAWINGS, PAINTINGS, WRITING, ENTRY TICKETS, PICTURES OR ALL THE OTHER STUFF YOU WANT TO CAPTURE

Date: _____   Place: _____

How I felt Today:

What I've Seen today:

_____
_____
_____
_____
_____
_____
_____
_____
_____
_____
_____
_____

What I Ate Today:

_____
_____
_____
_____

How did we Travel:

The Best Thing that happened tooday:

_____
_____

The Weather today was:

PLACE FOR DRAWINGS, PAINTINGS, WRITING, ENTRY TICKETS, PICTURES OR ALL THE OTHER STUFF YOU WANT TO CAPTURE

Date: | Place:

How I felt Today:

What I've Seen today:

_____
_____
_____
_____
_____
_____
_____
_____
_____
_____
_____

What I Ate Today:

_____
_____
_____
_____

How did we Travel:

The Best Thing that happened Tooday:

_____
_____

The Weather today was:

PLACE FOR DRAWINGS, PAINTINGS, WRITING, ENTRY TICKETS, PICTURES OR ALL THE OTHER STUFF YOU WANT TO CAPTURE

Date: Place:

How I felt Today:

What I've Seen today:

_____
_____
_____
_____
_____
_____
_____
_____
_____
_____
_____

What I Ate Today:

_____
_____
_____
_____

How did we Travel:

The Best Thing that happened tooday:
_____
_____

The Weather today was:

PLACE FOR DRAWINGS, PAINTINGS, WRITING, ENTRY TICKETS, PICTURES OR ALL THE OTHER STUFF YOU WANT TO CAPTURE

Date: _____ Place: _____

How I felt Today:

What I've Seen today:

_____
_____
_____
_____
_____
_____
_____
_____
_____
_____
_____

What I Ate Today:

_____
_____
_____
_____
_____

How did we Travel:

The Best Thing that happened tooday:

_____
_____

THe Weather today was:

PLACE FOR DRAWINGS, PAINTINGS, WRITING, ENTRY TICKETS, PICTURES OR ALL THE OTHER STUFF YOU WANT TO CAPTURE

DATE: PLACE:

HOW I FELT TODAY:

WHAT I'VE SEEN TODAY: WHAT I ATE TODAY:

_____   _____
_____   _____
_____   _____
_____   _____
_____   _____
_____
_____   HOW DID WE TRAVEL:
_____
_____
_____
_____
_____

THE BEST THING THAT HAPPENED TOODAY:
_____
_____

THE WEATHER TODAY WAS:

PLACE FOR DRAWINGS, PAINTINGS, WRITING, ENTRY TICKETS, PICTURES OR ALL THE OTHER STUFF YOU WANT TO CAPTURE

DATE: _____ PLACE: _____

HOW I FELT TODAY:

WHAT I'VE SEEN TODAY:

_____
_____
_____
_____
_____
_____
_____
_____
_____
_____
_____

WHAT I ATE TODAY:

_____
_____
_____
_____

HOW DID WE TRAVEL:

THE BEST THING THAT HAPPENED TOODAY:

_____
_____

THE WEATHER TODAY WAS:

PLACE FOR DRAWINGS, PAINTINGS, WRITING, ENTRY TICKETS, PICTURES OR ALL THE OTHER STUFF YOU WANT TO CAPTURE

Date:	Place:

How I felt Today:

What I've Seen today:	What I Ate Today:
_____	_____
_____	_____
_____	_____
_____	_____
_____	_____
_____	
_____	**How did we Travel:**
_____	
_____	
_____	
_____	

The Best Thing that happened tooday:
_____
_____

The Weather today was:

PLACE FOR DRAWINGS, PAINTINGS, WRITING, ENTRY TICKETS, PICTURES OR ALL THE OTHER STUFF YOU WANT TO CAPTURE

DATE: _____ PLACE: _____

HOW I FELT TODAY:

WHAT I'VE SEEN TODAY:

_____
_____
_____
_____
_____
_____
_____
_____
_____
_____
_____
_____

WHAT I ATE TODAY:

_____
_____
_____
_____

HOW DID WE TRAVEL:

THE BEST THING THAT HAPPENED TOODAY:
_____
_____

THE WEATHER TODAY WAS:

PLACE FOR DRAWINGS, PAINTINGS, WRITING, ENTRY TICKETS, PICTURES OR ALL THE OTHER STUFF YOU WANT TO CAPTURE

DATE: _____ | PLACE: _____

HOW I FELT TODAY:

WHAT I'VE SEEN TODAY:

_____
_____
_____
_____
_____
_____
_____
_____
_____
_____
_____

WHAT I ATE TODAY:

_____
_____
_____
_____

HOW DID WE TRAVEL:

THE BEST THING THAT HAPPENED TOODAY:

_____
_____

THE WEATHER TODAY WAS:

PLACE FOR DRAWINGS, PAINTINGS, WRITING, ENTRY TICKETS, PICTURES OR ALL THE OTHER STUFF YOU WANT TO CAPTURE

DATE: PLACE:

HOW I FELT TODAY:

WHAT I'VE SEEN TODAY:

_____
_____
_____
_____
_____
_____
_____
_____
_____
_____

WHAT I ATE TODAY:

_____
_____
_____
_____

HOW DID WE TRAVEL:

THE BEST THING THAT HAPPENED TOODAY:
_____
_____

THE WEATHER TODAY WAS:

PLACE FOR DRAWINGS, PAINTINGS, WRITING, ENTRY TICKETS, PICTURES OR ALL THE OTHER STUFF YOU WANT TO CAPTURE

Date: | Place:

HOW I FELT TODAY:

WHAT I'VE SEEN TODAY:

_____
_____
_____
_____
_____
_____
_____
_____
_____
_____
_____
_____

WHAT I ATE TODAY:

_____
_____
_____
_____

HOW DID WE TRAVEL:

THE BEST THING THAT HAPPENED TOODAY:

_____
_____

THE WEATHER TODAY WAS:

PLACE FOR DRAWINGS, PAINTINGS, WRITING, ENTRY TICKETS, PICTURES OR ALL THE OTHER STUFF YOU WANT TO CAPTURE

Date: | Place:

How I felt Today:

What I've Seen today:

_____
_____
_____
_____
_____
_____
_____
_____
_____
_____
_____
_____

What I Ate Today:

_____
_____
_____
_____

How did we Travel:

The Best Thing that happened tooday:

_____
_____

The Weather today was:

PLACE FOR DRAWINGS, PAINTINGS, WRITING, ENTRY TICKETS, PICTURES OR ALL THE OTHER STUFF YOU WANT TO CAPTURE

Date: _____   Place: _____

How I felt Today:

What I've Seen today:

_____
_____
_____
_____
_____
_____
_____
_____
_____
_____
_____

What I Ate Today:

_____
_____
_____
_____
_____

How did we Travel:

The Best Thing that happened tooday:

_____
_____

The Weather today was:

PLACE FOR DRAWINGS, PAINTINGS, WRITING, ENTRY TICKETS, PICTURES OR ALL THE OTHER STUFF YOU WANT TO CAPTURE

Date: _____   Place: _____

How I felt Today:

What I've Seen today:

_____
_____
_____
_____
_____
_____
_____
_____
_____
_____
_____
_____

What I Ate Today:

_____
_____
_____
_____
_____

How did we Travel:

The Best Thing that happened tooday:

_____
_____

The Weather today was:

PLACE FOR DRAWINGS, PAINTINGS, WRITING, ENTRY TICKETS, PICTURES OR ALL THE OTHER STUFF YOU WANT TO CAPTURE

Date: | Place:

How I felt Today:

What I've Seen today:	What I Ate Today:
_____	_____
_____	_____
_____	_____
_____	_____
_____	_____
_____	**How did we Travel:**
_____	
_____	
_____	
_____	
_____	

The Best Thing that happened tooday:
_____
_____

The Weather today was:

PLACE FOR DRAWINGS, PAINTINGS, WRITING, ENTRY TICKETS, PICTURES OR ALL THE OTHER STUFF YOU WANT TO CAPTURE

Date: Place:

How I felt Today:

What I've Seen today:

_____
_____
_____
_____
_____
_____
_____
_____
_____
_____
_____

What I Ate Today:

_____
_____
_____
_____
_____

How did we Travel:

The Best Thing that happened tooday:
_____
_____

The Weather today was:

PLACE FOR DRAWINGS, PAINTINGS, WRITING, ENTRY TICKETS, PICTURES OR ALL THE OTHER STUFF YOU WANT TO CAPTURE

jonathan kuhla
tempelhofer ufer 15
109 63 berlin
mail: jonathankuhla@gmail.com